LIGHTNING BOLT BOOKS

Dangerous Tornadoes

Lola Schaefer

Lerner Publications • Minneapolis

Thank you, Jason
Thistlethwaite,
University of
Waterloo

Lerner Publications Company
An imprint of Lerner Publishing Group, Inc.
241 First Avenue North
Minneapolis, MN 55401 USA

For reading levels and more information, look up this title at www.lernerbooks.com.

Main body text set in Billy Infant Regular. Typeface provided by SparkType.

Editor: Rebecca Higgins **Photo Editor:**
Lerner team: Sue Marquis

Library of Congress Cataloging-in-Publication Data

Names: Schaefer, Lola M., 1950- author.
Title: Dangerous tornadoes / Lola Schaefer.
Description: Minneapolis : Lerner Publications , [2022] | Series: Lightning bolt books - Earth in danger | Includes bibliographical references and index. | Audience: Ages 6-9 | Audience: Grades 2-3 | Summary: "Over 1,000 tornadoes touch down in the US every year. Readers learn the science behind the storm, how climate change impacts it, and how to stay safe during a tornado warning"— Provided by publisher.
Identifiers: LCCN 2021022621 (print) | LCCN 2021022622 (ebook) | ISBN 9781728441399 (library binding) | ISBN 9781728447964 (paperback) | ISBN 9781728444857 (ebook)
Subjects: LCSH: Tornadoes—Juvenile literature. | Tornadoes—Safety measures—Juvenile literature.
Classification: LCC QC955.2 .S36 2022 (print) | LCC QC955.2 (ebook) | DDC 551.55/3—dc23

LC record available at https://lccn.loc.gov/2021022621
LC ebook record available at https://lccn.loc.gov/2021022622

Manufactured in the United States of America
1-49910-49753-7/21/2021

Table of Contents

Tornadoes Twist

Storm clouds cover the sky. The wind blows and hail falls. A funnel-shaped cloud forms and rotates.

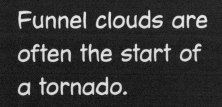

Funnel clouds are often the start of a tornado.

The cloud twists as winds push up. Its tail touches down. A roar fills the air. The tornado destroys objects in its path.

A tornado, sometimes called a twister, is a cloud that forms in a supercell. As it moves, rotating winds swirl upward.

Tornadoes pick up dirt and debris. Most tornadoes touch the ground for one to five minutes. A few stay down for one to three hours.

Tornadoes can carry debris for miles.

How Tornadoes Begin

Scientists don't know exactly how or why tornadoes begin. But they know that moisture, wind, lift, and unstable air are needed to make a tornado.

Warm, wet air formed these puffy clouds.

Climate change warms temperatures. Warmer air holds more water. When warm, wet air is next to the ground and cold, dry air is above it, the air becomes unstable.

An updraft is an early sign of a storm.

An updraft happens when warm, wet air meets cold, dry air. The warm air lifts, or rises, through the cold air.

When winds change speed and direction over a short distance, it is called wind shear. Wind shear and warm, moist air begin the movement that becomes a tornado.

Wind shears and instability create tornadoes.

Dangerous Tornadoes

The United States has more than one thousand tornadoes each year. These storms can be very dangerous.

Anemometers measure wind speed.

Tornadoes are rated on the Enhanced Fujita (EF) scale from 0 through 5. A 0 tornado can have winds as high as 85 miles (137 km) per hour. A 5 tornado can have winds as high as 300 miles (483 km) per hour.

The updraft of tornadoes does the most damage. Tornadoes uproot trees or throw cars. They dig up dirt and tear apart buildings.

Wet soil makes it easier for tornadoes to uproot trees.

Fallen power lines are very dangerous. Do not go near them and call 911.

Tornadoes can harm people and animals. Broken pieces of buildings or power poles fly through the air. These can strike, hurt, and even kill someone who is outside.

Staying Safe

Tornadoes cannot be prevented. But weather forecasters use Doppler radar to follow supercell storms. They warn people when these storms are near.

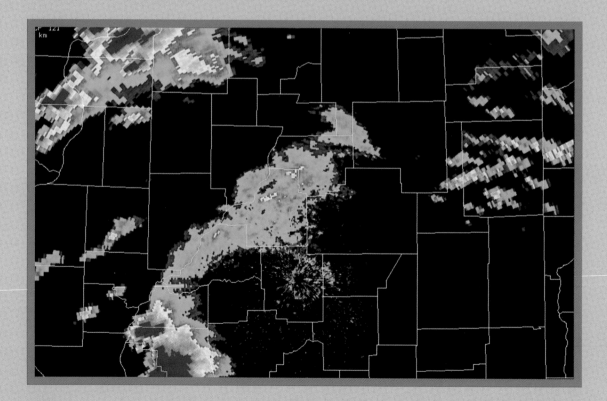

Sirens alert people to potential weather danger.

During a tornado watch, people need to be ready to take shelter. Listen to weather forecasters for updates on the tornado's path.

Schools often have students crouch with their heads down during a tornado drill.

Do not go outside to see a tornado. Stay inside and go to a basement or the lowest floor in a building. Go to a room with no windows. If you cannot go to a lower floor, go to a bathroom or closet.

Remain inside until you hear that it is safe. Tornadoes are part of nature. We can't stop them, but we can be prepared.

Cool air can weaken a tornado.

I Survived a Tornado

On May 20, 2013, professional storm chaser Amy Castor tracked a destructive tornado through Moore, Oklahoma. Castor watched as the tornado tore apart homes, businesses, and schools. Castor stayed three blocks away behind the tornado as she sent live video to her news station. The station showed the video so people knew to take shelter. Castor survived the tornado and helped others do so.

Tornado Facts

- Most tornadoes in North America spin counterclockwise. A few turn clockwise.

- Tornadoes have been recorded on every continent except Antarctica.

- In March 1925, the Tri-State Tornado swept through the Midwest for three and a half hours. It went from Missouri to Illinois to Indiana.

- Tornado Alley is an area in the southern plains of the central United States that has a high number of tornadoes in the spring.

Glossary

climate change: long-term changes in global temperature due to human and natural activity

debris: scattered pieces of something that has been broken

destroy: to damage or ruin

prevent: to stop something from happening

rotate: to move around a center point

supercell: a system that makes thunderstorms with rotating winds due to an updraft

updraft: when warm air rises until it condenses during the beginning of a storm

weather forecaster: someone who studies weather and tells others what the weather is likely to be

Learn More

Ducksters: Tornadoes
https://www.ducksters.com/science/earth
_science/tornadoes.php

Gibbons, Gail. *Tornadoes!* New York: Holiday House, 2019.

National Geographic Kids: Tornado
https://kids.nationalgeographic.com/science
/article/tornado

National Geographic Kids: Tornado Facts!
https://www.natgeokids.com/au/discover
/geography/physical-geography/tornado-facts/

Schaefer, Lola. *Dangerous Hurricanes.* Minneapolis: Lerner Publications, 2022.

Yolen, Jane, and Heidi E. Y. Stemple. *I Am the Storm.* New York: Rise x Penguin Workshop, 2020.

Index

Photo Acknowledgments

Image credits: Just Me/flickr (CC BY-SA 2.0), p. 4; Justin Hobson/Wikimedia Commons (CC BY-SA 3.0), p. 5; Chad Cowan/500px Prime/Getty Images, p. 6; ROSS TUCKERMAN/ AFP via Getty Images, p. 7; FrameStockFootages/Shutterstock.com, p. 8; John D Sirlin/ Shutterstock.com, p. 9; Lamax/Shutterstock.com, p. 10; Mike Hollingshead/Corbis Documentary/Getty Images, p. 11; inhauscreative/E+/Getty Images, p. 12; Wattanasit Chunopas/Shutterstock.com, p. 13; dcwcreations/Shutterstock.com, p. 14; KanitChurem/ Shutterstock.com, p. 15; NOAA/NWS, p. 16; Frank Anusewicz/Shutterstock.com, p. 17; AP Photo/Journal Times, Scott Anderson, p. 18; Mike Mareen/Shutterstock.com, p. 19.

Cover: solarseven/Shutterstock.com.